NORAH M. TITLEY

Sports and Pastimes

SCENES FROM TURKISH, PERSIAN
AND MUGHAL PAINTINGS

THE BRITISH LIBRARY

BRITISH LIBRARY BOOKLETS

It is the aim of this series of booklets to introduce the British Library to the general public by drawing attention to many fascinating aspects of its collections which are of interest to the layman as well as the scholar. Many of the items mentioned and illustrated in the booklets are frequently on exhibition in the British Library's exhibition galleries in the British Museum building in Great Russell Street, London W.C.1.

Published by the British Library,
Great Russell Street, London WC1B 3DG
🔖 British Library Cataloguing in Publication Data
Titley, Norah M
    Sports and pastimes
    1. British Library. Department of Oriental Manuscripts and
    Printed books
    2. Illumination of books and manuscripts, Islamic
    3. Miniature painting, Islamic   4. Recreation in Art
    I. Title   II. British Library. Reference Division
    751.7′7′0917671   ND2955
    ISBN 0-904654-10-9
Designed by Peter Campbell
Set in Monotype Garamond
Printed in Great Britain by
Oxley Press (Nottingham) Ltd.

Introduction

The British Library, in its collection in the Department of Oriental Manuscripts and Printed Books, has some of the finest Persian and Mughal illustrated manuscripts ever produced as well as one of the best collections of illustrated Turkish manuscripts outside Istanbul. This booklet is one of a series intended to introduce the visitor (both actual and armchair) to the British Library's collections by allowing the manuscripts to speak for themselves. The sports and pastimes described in this small book are all to be seen in miniatures in manuscripts from Persia, Turkey and Mughal India and as many as possible are included in the illustrations. The history of Persian and Turkish art is not discussed here because booklets on the subject have already been produced by the British Library.

All the illustrations in this booklet are taken from manuscripts in the British Library and some of these manuscripts are usually on exhibition. Similar manuscripts are also often on exhibition in other museums and libraries such as in Paris (Bibliothèque Nationale), Berlin (Dahlem Museum), New York (Metropolitan Museum of Art) and Dublin (Chester Beatty Library and Gallery of Oriental Art). They can also be seen elsewhere in England in the galleries of the Victoria and Albert Museum (London), the Fitzwilliam Museum (Cambridge) and the Bodleian Library (Oxford).

Persian, Turkish and Mughal manuscripts often contain miniatures showing a wide variety of recreational pursuits. These range from celebrations, banquets and picnics through comparatively tranquil games such as backgammon and chess to the mounted archery contests which were used as cavalry training. Most illustrated manuscripts of epics, histories, poems, glossaries and encyclopaedic works included paintings which showed people being entertained or taking part in some pastime or other. Works by Persian, Indian and Turkish poets such as Niẓāmī, Saʿdī, Ḥāfiẓ, Amīr Khusraw and Nevāʾī not only include accounts of actual wrestling bouts, games of polo, hunting, music and other recreations in their poems but use them in the elaborate imagery which is such a feature of their literature. An artist illustrating an anthology of poems would select a single line as the subject of a miniature even if it only obliquely referred to a polo match or other recreation.

The epic poem, the *Shāhnāma* (Book of Kings), which the Persian poet Firdawsī completed in over fifty thousand rhyming couplets in AD 1010 abounds with accounts of polo, hunting, chess, backgammon, archery, wrestling, celebrations, music and feasting as well as contests of one kind or another. The *Shāhnāma* related the legend and history of the four Iranian dynasties up to the Islamic invasions in the seventh century AD ending with the death of the last Sasanian king, Yazdigard III, in 652–3. Persian manuscripts of the *Shāhnāma* date from the fourteenth century onwards. The work was also copied and illustrated in India during the Mughal period when Persian was the court language. Illustrated copies in the original Persian or in Turkish translation were also produced in Turkey from the sixteenth century onwards. The multitudinous stories and anecdotes provide a wealth of subject-matter which allow an artist to give full rein to his imagination.

POLO

The game of polo (*chawgān*) which is reputed to have originated in Persia, is often the subject of miniatures. Manuscript illustrations do not show more than eight players and more often than not there are only four or six, although accounts of European travellers in the late sixteenth and the seventeenth centuries, such as Sir William Shirley and Sir John Chardin, tell of twelve, fifteen or even twenty players taking part. The main protagonists are set in prominent positions in the centre. The goalposts are often drawn in, sometimes painted in gold as is the ball, and pages (*payks*) on foot are shown standing in strategic positions in the foreground holding spare sticks to replace those which get broken. Onlookers and, sometimes, drummers and trumpeters stand in the background half-hidden in the landscape.

Shah Abbās I (1586–1628) who made Isfahan his capital created the *maydān-i shāh*, the huge square near the bazaar, and would sit high up in his royal pavilion overlooking it to watch the activities which took place there including polo, which he himself often played. Shirley spoke of polo at the time as 'a game of great difficulty . . . their horses are so well trained to this that they run after the ball like cats. . . .' However, polo, which spread from Iran to China and Turkey and was taken to India by the Mongols, was a royal sport long before the seventeenth century. It was played to the accompaniment of drums and trumpets and in descriptions of games it is likened to a battle with the beating of drums, the shouts of the players and the neighing of the horses which raised thick clouds of dust under their thundering hoofs.

In the *Shāhnāma* Firdawsī describes polo matches as a test in which a hero proves his ability and strength as, for instance, in the story of Siyāvush who, demonstrating his prowess, 'mounted a fresh horse, threw up the ball and drove it out of sight to see the moon.' Firdawsī also tells the story of a polo game on foot when the king Ardashīr, who had never seen Shāpūr, his seven year old son, devised a game which included the boy amongst one hundred others of similar age and appearance. The king ordered the ball to be thrown into the field towards him knowing that only his son would dare to follow it. His plan was successful for all the other boys hung back and Shāpūr ran after the ball close to where his father was sitting.

Besides the accounts in the *Shāhnāma* and the allusions to polo in single lines of poetry, romantic poems sometimes describe polo games in detail. Two of these are *Khusraw va Shīrīn*, one of the five poems of the *Khamsa* of Niẓāmī (d. *ca.* 1203) and *Shīrīn va Khusraw* by the Indian poet Amīr Khusraw (d. 1325), who modelled his five poems (*Khamsa*) on those of Niẓāmī. The poems tell of the love of the Iranian ruler Khusraw Parvīz for the Armenian princess Shīrīn, of their eventual meeting on the hunting grounds and the polo match they played against each other with their respective companions completing the teams. Shīrīn, accompanied by her women companions, delighted to take part in masculine pursuits such as hunting and polo and her match against Khusraw is often the subject of miniatures illustrating the *Khamsa* (fig. 8). Another romantic poem, that of *Mihr va Mushtarī* by 'Aṣṣār (d. *ca.* 1382) which describes the banishment of Mihr from his father's kingdom whence he fled to the country of the kings of Kayvan where he had to prove himself by his skill at polo. The Persian poet Sa'dī (d. 1292) composed moral anecdotes as well as poems and illustrated copies of his collected works (*Kulliyāt*) usually include polo scenes. Manuscripts of these works and others were copied in India and illustrated in the Mughal style particularly during the reign of the great patron of the art of the book, the Mughal emperor Akbar (d. 1605). His son Jahāngīr (d. 1627) was a patron also and a manuscript of the poems of Ḥāfiẓ (Or. 7573) includes a miniature to illustrate a line of a poem alluding to polo and, as a compliment to his royal patron, the artist has painted the four players in the likeness of Jahāngīr and his three sons. Another Mughal manuscript, part of the *Dārābnāma* dated *ca.* 1580 (Or. 4615), has three polo miniatures to illustrate the story of the queen, Humāy, playing polo with her slaves against an opponent who dominated the game until Humāy's son Dārāb galloped onto the field and, taking the ball the length of the ground, scored a goal. A manuscript of the *Khāvarānnāma* by Muhammad ibn Husām, which has miniatures in the Panjabi style (Add. 19766) dated 1686, is a fanciful prose account of the exploits of 'Alī and his companions in which they visit strange lands and places. Amongst these places is the City of Gold which was guarded by gold talis-manic polo players. Polo is used extensively in imagery by poets such as 'Umar Khayyām and Niẓāmī, an example being the latter's advice on how to live a full life: 'The horizon is the boundary of your polo ground, the earth is the ball in the curve of your polo stick. Until the dust of non-existence rises from annihilation, gallop and urge on your horse because the ground is yours'.

HUNTING

Hunting occurs over and over again in the *Shāhnāma* (Book of Kings) and every illustrated copy of the work from the fourteenth century onwards has its hunting scenes. One of the finest descriptions occurs in the account of Khusraw Parvīz setting out to hunt and the wealth of detail given in such incidents explains why the *Shāhnāma* stories so often proved to be an inspiration and challenge to artists. The story of Khusraw and Shīrīn occurs in the *Shāhnāma*, as well as in the poem by Niẓāmī mentioned above, and with his usual splendid exaggeration. Firdawsī evokes a glittering scene of preparations for a hunting expedition. He describes three hundred horses, covered in caparisons of gold, which were taken for Khusraw and the thousand men, some of whom carried two-headed darts, whilst others had swords and who all wore brocade over their coats of mail. There were seven hundred falconers with royal falcons, sparrow hawks and gos-hawks and behind them came mounted men, three hundred keepers of cheetahs. Besides the cheetahs there were seventy leopards and lions all harnessed with Chinese brocade, all trained for hunting and wearing gold muzzles. For the deer hunt there were eight hundred hounds with golden leashes. Behind these animals came two thousand minstrels with harps all on camels and crowned with gold. Five hundred more camels went ahead carrying seats, pavilions and tent enclosures and two hundred slaves went with them to light censers for burning sweetscented aloewood and ambergris. Two hundred youths attended the king (Khusraw) carrying bunches of saffron and narcissus so that the scent might waft to him from all quarters as he travelled, himself preceded by one hundred water-bearers whose task it was to lay the dust by sprinklng water on the road. Khusraw, with whom three hundred princes rode, wore a crown and earrings and a cloth-of-gold tunic with a gold belt and armlets and jewelled buttons.

As far as they were able, within the confines of a page, artists of the sumptuous Persian Safavid manuscripts of the sixteenth century and of Mughal miniatures of Akbar's time as well as the late six-teenth century Turkish miniaturists (fig. 9) have been very successful in portraying the splendour of the hunt. Sometimes hunting in Mongol fashion (*jirgeh*) is depicted in which a circular 'stockade' is constructed into which the beaters drive game. Hunting takes place by order of rank, first the king, then the princes and next the nobles and so on in turn. Sometimes game is encircled by a sold phalanx of men who serve as the stockade fence. Illustrated manuscripts of the memoirs or diaries of Bābur, the first Mughal emperor (d. 1530), usually contain several miniatures of hunting including the *jirgeh* method as do Ottoman Turkish manuscripts in which hunting is described. In Persian manuscripts cheetahs are sometimes shown carried on horseback on a pad attached to the cantle of the saddle behind the rider but in Mughal miniatures cheetahs are usually carried, blindfolded, on a flat ox-cart or else on a platform suspended by ropes from a pole carried by two men. Hounds such as salukis often occur, sometimes led by men on foot but usually running free. Falcons and hawks are much in evidence and, when single paintings became the vogue in the late sixteenth and seventeenth century in Persian, Mughal and Turkish art, portraits of favourite birds, often wearing hoods and jesses (leg harness), were painted. The goshawk appears most frequently in Turkish miniatures, complete with the halsband or narrow strip of leather round its neck (fig. 1.). One convention of Persian and Turkish hunting scenes is that of the lion skulking behind reeds and another is the bear standing on its hind legs high up on the mountains hurling a rock at the huntsmen below. All manner of weapons are used, spears, bows and arrows, lances, swords and even bare hands as when a huntsman is shown astride a lion forcing its jaws open. Other examples of hunting prowess include catching an animal by lassoing or by looping a bow round its neck and, occasionally, by running on foot beside it to pull it down.

The exploits of the famous hunter Bahrām Gūr are related by Niẓāmī in another of the poems included in his *Khamsa*, the *Haft Paykar* (Seven Portraits), as well as by Firdawsī in the *Shāhnāma*. Bahrām Gūr took the maiden called by Niẓāmī, Fitna (Mischief) and by Firdawsī, Azāda, with him when he went hunting. Sometimes she is shown riding a horse and sometimes sitting behind Bahram Gūr on a camel or dromedary, but she is always playing a harp. This incident appears on metal work dating from Sasanian times and on twelfth- and thirteenth-century ceramics and in miniatures from the fourteenth century onwards. Fitna or Azāda infuriated Bahrām Gūr by her seeming indifference to his hunting prowess, merely remarking 'practice makes perfect' after he had performed a particularly skilful feat of marksmanship. In his rage and wounded pride he hurled her to the ground and rode over her and demanded her execution. She was, however, smuggled away and some two years later was able to get even with him as, unrecognised, she carried a fully-grown ox on her shoulders upstairs before him murmuring 'practice makes perfect' in the face of his astonishment. The incidents in this story are often illustrated, showing Fitna or Azāda playing the harp, Bahrām Gūr demonstrating his archery skill, the girl being trampled upon and, finally, carrying the ox on her shoulders upstairs and poets often include it in the imagery of their poetry. Miniatures of hunting scenes sometimes received very special treatment as in a sixteenth-century Shiraz manuscript of the *Ẓafarnāma* (Book of Victories) (Add. 7635), the history of Tīmūr, in which the mountains are decorated with mother-of-pearl. In the hunting scene used as a frontispiece to a volume of poems (Or. 11388) the quivers and saddlecloths are encrusted with what appears to be crushed semi-precious stones.

ARCHERY

The skill of the archer is well portrayed in hunting scenes but archery contests and target practice are sometimes the sole subject of miniatures. In Turkey archery was a national sport and contests were held in which mounted archers at full gallop aimed at a small target such as a brass ball or upturned flask on a high pole (fig. 2). The illustration comes from a Turkish manuscript, a *Dīvān* (anthology) of the poems of 'Alī Ṣīr Nevā'ī (d. 1501), and shows very clearly the way a contest was conducted. It would take place, as illustrated, on the archery ground (*ok meydān*), to the accompaniment of drums, trumpets and shawms (short trumpets) and whilst horsemen in the foreground awaited their turn, others galloped round the pole aiming at the ball or flask, while pages on foot kept the horsemen supplied with arrows. Originally a gourd (*qabaq*) was used as a target but later a brass ball or bowl or flask was substituted. All the miniatures in this volume of poems (Or. 5346), which dates from the mid-sixteenth century, are concerned with recreation and pastimes of one kind or another including hunting, polo and entertainment out of doors as well as the archery contest. De Busbecq who was imperial ambassador at Constantinople from 1554 to 1562 during the reign of Suleymān the Magnificent (d. 1566) has given a very interesting account of contemporary Turkey in a series of letters. He described the Turkish archery contests as an old custom going back to the Parthians in which they pretended to flee and then turned in their saddles to shoot the pursuing enemy. 'They practice the rapid execution of this device in the following manner. They fix a brazen ball on the top of a very high pole or mast, erected on level ground, and urge their horses at full speed towards the mast and then, when they

1 *Goshawk wearing jesse, bells and halsband*

Or. 2709 (folio 21a).
From an album.
Turkish.
Sixteenth century.

have almost passed it, they suddenly turn round and, leaning back, discharge an arrow at the ball, while the horse continues on its course. By frequent practice they became able, without any difficulty, to hit their enemy unawares by shooting backwards as they fly.' Another contemporary account, this time of an archery contest on the *maydān* at Isfahan is that by the French traveller Chardin of a

similar method of shooting backwards at a golden ball fixed on a high pole.

An eighteenth-century manuscript of a Persian translation of the Hindu epic the *Mahābhārata* (Add. 5638) has miniatures in the provincial Mughal style of Muradabad including one of the archery contest which took place for the hand of Draupadī. Arjuna successfully hit the target, the left eye of the fish mounted on a high pole, by looking at its reflection in a cauldron of oil placed on the ground.

WRESTLING

Wrestling is another martial sport of which contests were often described and illustrated. Wrestling bouts, as in the case of polo matches, are sometimes the subject of a fairly long story or sometimes briefly referred to in a single line of poetry. Sa'dī (d. 1292) used wrestling in several of his moral tales and the story most frequently illustrated is that of the old wrestler who knew three hundred and sixty tricks but withheld the secret of one of them from his arrogant young pupil. When the young man attempted to prove his superiority over the old master during a wrestling bout held before the king, the old man defeated him by the secret hold (fig. 3) and Sa'dī drew the moral that a person should not allow anyone, even a friend, to know everything about himself as, should that person become an enemy, he would hold him in his power. Sa'dī also used archery to emphasize his argument and told of the man who brought up a youth as his own son and when the boy turned against him he said 'I never taught a novice how to shoot but, in the end, he drew his bow against me.'

The art of wrestling is to be seen, together with traditional gymnastics exercises, in Iran to this day in the *Zūrkhāna* or 'house of strength'. The tight-fitting breeches of leather or other strong material worn by the wrestlers are in the same tradition as those of early Islamic times and exercises are performed to drumbeats and recitations. A manuscript dated AD 1800 in the British Library (Or. 1370) has a miniature showing wrestlers in the traditional *zūrkhāna* costume. The ancient art of wrestling is vividly described by Firdawsī in the *Shāhnāma* particularly the contest between Rustam and Pūlādvand (fig. 4). This occurred during a battle between the Turanians and Iranians in the war which forms the central theme through so much of the *Shāhnāma*. The Turanian king, Afrāsiyāb, finding the tide of the battle turning against him, appealed to the demon king Pūlādvand for assistance. Pūlādvand left his mountain kingdom in China taking an army with him and put the

Iranian troops to flight. The mighty Rustam stood his ground and faced Pūlādvand single-handed, hitting him so violently with his mace that he expected 'the brains of Pūlādvand to pour from both his ears.' Neither could overcome the other, either with mace or sword, so Pūlādvand challenged Rustam to a wrestling-match, saying '. . . wrestling is the test 'twixt man and man. Take we each other by the leathern belt, that we may know which one the will of fate dismisseth worsted from the battlefield.' Rustam accepted the challenge and defeated Pūlādvand who withdrew his army and returned to his own kingdom leaving the Iranians to defeat Afrā-siyāb's army and to win this particular campaign.

3 *Wrestling*
Or. 5302 (folio 30a).
From the *Gulistān* of
Sa'dī. Persian
(Bukhara). 1567

4 *Rustam and
Pulādvand
wrestling*
Add. 18188 (folio
167a). From the
Shāhnāma of
Firdawsī. Persian
(Shiraz). 1486

PIGEONS

Besides the martial sports of polo, hunting, archery and wrestling there were other pursuits of a more peaceful nature. Pigeons were kept as a pastime and illustrated copies of the poem by Hilālī (d. 1528) *Shāh u Gudā* (the King and the Beggar) usually have miniatures of

علی شیرخلیفه

روی زمین بزور آوری روی بر من دست نیافت بلکه مرا در علم دقیقهٔ مانده بوده که

5 *Prince with his pigeons*

Or. 4124 (80a). From the *Shāh u Gudā* of Hilālī. Persian (Tabriz). 1550

the young prince and his pigeons. The miniature illustrated (fig. 5) shows him standing on the roof gazing at his flock which the artist has drawn in the margin flying high above the painting and which includes tumbler pigeons. These are a variety of domestic pigeon which turn over and over backwards during their flight.

Children's games are illustrated in a glossary copied at Malwa in western India *ca.* AD 1500. The manuscript is illustrated by a Persian artist imported into India by the Muslim ruler of the time. The work, the *Miftaḥ al-Fuẓalā* (Or. 3299) is a glossary of rare words and proper names occuring in ancient Persian poetry in which the Hindi and Arabic equivalents are also sometimes given. It contains over one hundred and eighty small miniatures illustrating words quoted in the text and the artist is outstandingly original, not only in the choice of words to illustrate, but also in the way he interprets them. It is particularly interesting from the point of view of children's games to see that they played with the same kind of toys still popular today. The word *farmuk* (folio 212b) (fig .6) meaning a spinning top or a yoyo is illustrated by two boys each of whom has one of the toys. Two games of filling the mouth with air and either striking the lips

6 *Spinning top and yoyo*
Or. 3299 (folio 212b). From the *Miftāh al-Fuzalā*, a glossary by Shādiyābādi. Malwa. *ca.* 1500

7 *Hobby horse*
Or. 3299 (folio 220b).
Details as for fig. 6.

کم و کاست و نقصان شد گشت تنخانه کبران و

ترسایان گرفت بلید کمیت شراب سرخ زرک

است کورشت بواو بارسی دمین جوب که بلدان

خوانند

کودکان بازی کسند و آزادهندوی زندا موهی

وقیل با کاف بارسی نیز خوانند گلت پانپان

گشت ازهم بازشد و شکست گلات دیهی

بریلندی باشدیامر کوپی آبادان و خراب گشت

(folio 199a) or the cheeks (folio 145b) in order to produce a noise are the same as those played by modern children in their Tarzan or Red Indian games. Hobby horses (fig. 7) in the form of sticks ridden

8 *Khusraw and Shīrīn playing polo*
Or. 2931 (folio 75a).
From the *Khamsa* of Niẓāmī. Persian.
AD1478

9 *Hunting*
Add. 15153 (folio
13b). From the
Humāyūnnāme.

10A *Tavern*
Or. 4125 (folio 109a)
Dīvān of Nevā'ī.
Turkish. Sixteenth
century.

10B *Maidens
discovered bathing*
Or. 12208 (folio
220a). *Khamsa* of
Niẓāmī. Mughal.
1593

11 *New Year*
(Nuruz) *Picnic*
Add. 15531 (folio
514a) *Shāhnāma* of
Firdawsī. Persian
(Tabriz). 1536

12 *Bābur celeb-
ing the birth o
heir Humāyūn
Or. 3714 (295a)
Vāqi'āt-i Bāburī
(the Memoirs o
Babur). Mugha
ca. 1590

طوی ولادت همایون شد امراو غیر امراخورد و کلان پلخونآوردند

13 *Swing*
Or. 3299 (folio 291a).
Details as for fig. 6.

by boys (folio 220b), a swing (fig. 13) (folio 291a) and a bull-roarer created by whirling leather on a double string (217a) are illustrated. There are also two pictures of dolls (fig. 14) (folios 51b and 260b) shown being played with by girls.

14 *Dolls*
Or. 3299 (folio 260b).
Details as for fig. 6.

15 (Top) *Automa-
ton of a king*
(Below) *Automaton
of a woman lighting
candles*
Or. 7968 (folio 102b)
'*Ajā'ib al-makhluqāt*
by Qazvīnī. Mughal.
seventeenth century.

16 *Automaton of a
horseman*
Or. 7968 (folio 102a)
'*Ajā'ib al-makhluqāt*
by Qazvini. Mughal
seventeenth century.

Far more sophisticated than the children's toys are the automata. Diagrams and paintings of these appear in a famous Arabic work *Kitāb fī ma'rifat al-ḥiyal al-handasiyya* (The Book of Knowledge of Ingenious Devices) by Ibn al-Razzāz al-Jazarī who was known, understandably, as Badī' al-Zamān (Prodigy of the Age). He completed the work in AD 1204 and there is a Persian translation of parts of it in the British Library. Al-Jazarī's source appears to have been a 9th-century Arabic work which drew its inspiration from the Greek writers Philon and Heron. Heron wrote about geography and also made clocks and other instruments of time whilst Philon was skilled in the construction of water-wheels, mills and ingenious devices. Some of the latter were playthings, some timepieces and others were connected with irrigation. Al-Jazarī divided his work into six categories including clocks and vessels and figures suitable for drinking sessions. The Persian translation of Jazarī's work was, like the glossary mentioned above, produced in Malwa in western India; it is dated 1509 and contains several diagrams of automata. There is also a section on automata in the encyclopaedic work, the *'Ajā'ib al-Makhlūqāt* (Wonders of Creation), an Arabic work by Qazvīnī. His work contains sections on astronomy, astrology, geography, animals, plants, birds and monsters as well as automata. Although Persian and Turkish translations have often been copied and illustrated, the section on automata is not usually illustrated. However one seventeenth-century manuscript (Or. 7968) in the British Library contains three illustrations of automata and one of a musical box. The latter contains four miniature tamburs (similar to a small lute) which play music when the mechanism is set in motion. One of the automata is of a horseman on a dome (fig. 16). According to the text the wine, which should be poured into the pipe, first reaches 'the cup of justice' and then turns a wheel which operates a spindle and causes the horseman to revolve. Of the other two, one is of a king seated in front of a pavilion. His servants pull the curtains and when the king sits down they stand and when the king stands they disappear (fig. 15). The other is of a woman who moves round the throne lighting candles with a taper.

CARD GAMES

Card games (*kanjīfa* or *ganjīfa*) were played in Iran, India and Turkey but do not appear to figure in miniatures. Indian cards were believed to be the earliest and there were normally ninety-six in a pack although one hundred and twenty were used in some games. They were generally of pasteboard, circular or oblong in shape and painted in bright colours. In his memoirs, Bābur (d. 1530), the first Mughal emperor of India, makes what is thought to be one of the earliest references to card games in oriental literature when he mentions that he sent playing cards (*ganjīfa*) to one Shāh Hasan in 1526.

17 *Chess*
Add. 16561 (folio 36b). Anthology of poems. Persian (Shirvan). 1468.

CHESS

Even if playing cards were not the subject of miniatures the same cannot be said about backgammon and, in particular, chess. As in polo and wrestling, moves in the games were used in the imagery of poetry as for example in a line in a poem by Kātibī (d.1435) (fig. 17) and also in a well-known verse in the Rubayyāt of 'Umar Khayyām, quoted here in the Fitzgerald version:

But helpless Pieces of the Game he plays
Upon this chequer-board of Nights and Days.
Hither and thither moves and checks and slays.
And one by one back in the closet lays.

Anecdotes and stories concerning chess occur in works by Sa'dī and the game also figures largely in the *Shāhnāma* in which Firdawsī describes the legendary invention of chess (*shatranj*) and backgammon (*nard*) at some length. One of the earliest references to *shatranj* occurs in a seventh-century Avestan work written in old Persian (*Pahlavi*) and it was this source that Firdawsī used in the *Shāhnāma* when describing how chess was sent as a challenge from India to Iran and how backgammon was sent to India in reply. The story of the invention of chess as told in the *Shāhnāma* concerns the half-brothers Gav and Talhand, sons of a queen of India, who became involved in a battle in which Gav died. Their mother ordered Talhand to explain how Gav met his end and Talhand consulted the sages as to the best way to do this. They had an ebony board made on which one hundred squares were cut and the two armies, one of teak and one of ivory, were drawn up face to face, each with a king (*shāh*) at the centre. The king's prime minister (the queen in the modern game) was at his side and next to them were two elephants bearing thrones. Then came two camels ridden by two men 'of holy counsel' (bishops); next to the camels came two cavalrymen (knights) and each wing ended in a warrior-rukh. The *rukh*, a mythical bird derived from the Chinese phoenix, is a fierce creature with plumes like flames. It attacked and killed rhinoceros and elephants for food. The rukh's move was always to advance until he had crossed the battlefield and reached the king. The minister could not move more than a single square from the king whereas the elephants, camels and horses could

move three squares. The warrior-rukh could move in every direction and charge across the battlefield at will. They all contended in their proper places and kept within their limits. When one saw the king fighting he would shout and the king would change his square until he was defeated. When the king's path was blocked on all sides and he could see his own men were overthrown and that the enemy were at his right and left, front and rear, and when he was unable to move in any direction he would die (*shāhmāt*) (checkmate). The battle itself between Gav and Talhand is sometimes the subject of a miniature in the *Shāhnāma* with the opposing armies carefully drawn up according to the description in the text.

BACKGAMMON

Firdawsī also relates the legend of the introduction of chess into Iran and the invention of backgammon (*nard*). During the reign of Anushīrvān (*Chosroe I*) the Raja of India sent an envoy to him with many gifts which included a chess set and board together with a letter challenging his sages to solve the rules of the game. Should they succeed the Raja pledged himself to send tribute to the court of Anushīrvān but if they failed then tribute must be sent to him. The Indian envoy unwittingly gave a clue by saying it was a war game but even so the sages were baffled by it, all except Anushīrvān's wise minister, Buzurjmihr, who, after studying it for a day and a night, solved its mysteries. Not only did he solve chess but he invented *nard* (backgammon) to be despatched to the Raja on terms which differed from the original only in that the Raja must pay double tribute if his wise men could not solve the rules of the game. Buzurjmihr, when inventing backgammon:

> ... bade to make two dice of ivory
> With dots the colour of teak-wood thereon,
> Arrayed a field of battle as in chess,
> And drew up the opposing hosts for war,
> Arranging them in eight battalions,
> All ready for pitched battle or for sieges.
> The ground was dark, the battlefield foursquare,
> Two noble clement kings were in command,
> Who had a common movement on the field,
> But neither sought the other's injury.
> The troops arrayed beneath their leadership
> For battle on both sides, were keen for fight
> If two friends catch an unsupported foe,
> The two inflict defeat upon the one.
> He made the two kings move about the field
> In pomp surrounded by their several hosts,

Each wheeling round about upon the other,
And combating by turns on hill and plain.
In this wise till one side was overthrown
The armies of both monarchs kept the field.
(Warner, *The Shāhnāma of Firdawsi*,
    Volume VII, p. 389)

No one amongst the Indian sages was able to solve the game and double tribute was duly sent to Anushīrvān. A manuscript of the *Shāhnāma* (Add. 15531) in the British Library has a miniature of Buzurjmihr inventing backgammon with the use of compasses whilst the Indian envoys, their chessboard on the ground, sit

18 *Backgammon*
Or. 3299 (folio 184a).
Details as for fig. 6.

19 *Backgammon*
Or. 3299 (folio 144a).
Details as for fig. 6.

watching him. The Malwa glossary (Or. 3299) which illustrates children's games also has two miniatures concerned with backgammon (figs. 18 – 19).

CELEBRATIONS

In scenes of celebrations, whether victories, accessions of kings, births, weddings or the New Year, wine is usually in evidence. This is also true of parties held indoors or in gardens or out in the countryside. *Sāqīs* (cupbearers) offer cups of wine to the king and the lover shares one with his beloved while flasks are carried in and wine cups are filled by attendants. Taverns, too, are a subject for illustration (fig. 10A). Sometimes the tavern and wine are referred to in a realistic sense as in the *Shāhnāma*, sometimes they are symbolic as, for example, in the Rubayyāt of 'Umar Khayyām and in the poems of Ḥāfiẓ and Jalāl al-Dīn Rūmī. In the poems of the mystics wine is the symbol of ecstasy or mystic love, the lover is man, the Beloved is God, the vintner is the teacher of mystic love and the tavern the place where it was taught. In illustrated manuscripts the artist usually illustrates such poems literally as in the anthology of the poems of 'Ali Şir Neva'i (d. 1501) (or 4125) (fig. 10A) who wrote in the Chagatay (Turki) language as well as in Persian and whose works were translated into Ottoman Turkish and served as models to later Ottoman poets. Poems entitled the *Sāqīnāma* (Book of the Cupbearer) have been composed since the fourteenth century, so many, in fact, that they have been referred to occasionally as the 'inevitable' *Sāqīnāma* in literary histories of Iran, Turkey and India. The Turkish poet Riyāzī (d. 1644) included a line in a poem on spring which illustrates the imagery conjured up by wine: 'The *sāqī* again sheds roses from the collar of the flask' – the 'roses' being the red wine and the 'collar' the neck of the flask.

However, all descriptions of wine were not metaphorical and in his memoirs Bābur (d. 1530) describes wine parties which were held, upon one pretext or another, in camps, gardens, palaces and even boats. These memoirs (*Vāqi'āt-i Bāburī*) originally written in Turki were translated into Persian and copiously illustrated manuscripts were copied particularly in the time of Bābur's grandson Akbar (d. 1605) who was one of the greatest patrons of the book. A copy in the British Library (Or. 3714) dated *ca*. 1590 contains over ninety miniatures and several of these are concerned with Bābur's celebration parties held to welcome envoys, celebrate births, victories, reunions and so on. Bābur's recreations were wide-ranging and his capacity for enjoyment apparently limitless. He is one of the great diarists of the world and in spite of all his campaigns and his turbulent military and political life he still found time to keep his diary. He describes in minute detail the animals and birds seen on his travels as well as the gardens he planned and had laid out. His account of hunting, entertainments and parties and, not least, the descriptions of his guests were lively and perceptive. He succeeded his father when only twelve years old in 1494, became the first Mughal emperor of India in 1526 (Mughal is a corruption of Mongol – a reference to Bābur's antecedents) and died in Agra in December 1530. One of his parties was held to celebrate the birth of his eldest son Humāyūn in 1508 and he ends his description with: 'It was a first-rate feast.' It took place in the Chāhār-Bāgh, a garden laid out by Bābur at Kabul and the artist of the miniature (Sūr Gujarātī) (fig. 12) has very successfully conveyed the joyous nature of the occasion and the lovely garden setting in which the party was held. Bābur is seated on a carpet beneath a canopy, leaning, propped up by a cushion, against the trunk of a plane tree (*chenār*) whilst a servant offers him a dish and musicians play. A man flourishing swords and a girl with castanets dance before him near a fountain while, in the foreground, envoys arrive with gifts.

GARDENS

Gardens were a source of unfailing pleasure and recreation to Bābur and also to several of his descendants. Before going to India Bābur spent some twenty years in Afghanistan and laid out gardens near Kabul. He goes into considerable detail in his memoirs as to the plan of the gardens and the systems of irrigation besides descriptions of the plants and trees. One of his abiding pleasures was creating new gardens or altering established ones, straightening the course of a stream here, planting imported trees and flowers there. Plane trees which he originally planted were described some three hundred years later as still flourishing. He was buried according to his wishes in a terraced garden at Kabul overlooking the plains and hills. It was during his grandson Akbar's reign that gardens at Srinagar in Kashmir were created on the lovely site round Lake Dhal and by the time Akbar's son Jahāngīr came to the throne in 1605 it is reported that there were seven hundred such gardens. Jahāngīr inherited his great-grandfather's interest in recording all his activities and also his love of gardens. He created the Shalimar Gardens in Kashmir and his wife Nūrjahān laid out the Dilkusha (heart-delighting) gardens near Lahore. Shāhjahān who succeeded Jahāngīr in 1627 visited the gardens at Kabul and laid one out there himself.

Some of the most beautiful Persian miniatures are those in which gardens form the background of festivities. Plants and trees are invariably in full bloom, the sky is gold or deep lapis lazuli blue and water flows in a stream between flowered banks or in channels to a central pool and fountain. In contrast to the heat and dust of the desert the garden has been likened to Paradise from time immemorial. In poetry it is a constantly recurring theme and this is reflected in the romantic art of the Persian miniaturist. Gardens were the setting for banquets, music, chess, story telling, courtship and philosophical arguments to mention only a few of the many activities which took place in them. Plane trees, cypresses, poplars, orange and pomegranate trees, hollyhocks, violets, peonies, day lilies, irises and, inevitably, roses all occur in the miniatures and in the imagery of poems. A lovely example of a fourteenth-century miniature of an idyllic garden scene shows the lovers, Humāy and Humāyūn, being entertained with music and wine in a glorious setting (fig. 20). Birds are circling in the golden sky, roses are being gathered, the lovers hold hands whilst beautiful maidens sit on the ground amongst flowering plants of all descriptions. A stream flows in the foreground between banks of flowers and musicians play nearby. The Persian garden, the theme of so many arts, is brought into the house in the form of the carpet designs. These 'garden' carpets have flower beds divided by channels of water, trees at each corner, a central pool with fish and ducks and everywhere in the pattern there are flowers.

20 *Humāy and Humāyūn entertained in a garden*
Add. 18113 (40b) *Humāy u Humāyūn* by Khvāju Kirmāni. Persian (Baghdad). 1396.

At the beginning of manuscripts there is sometimes a double-page painting of a prince or noble, possibly the artist's patron. Usually, on the right-hand page, he is being entertained by music and wine while, on the opposite page, a banquet is being prepared. Cauldrons are heated and stirred over fires between stones, dough is rolled, sticks gathered, fruit put in bowls, wine flasks filled and dishes carried in under the supervision of the steward complete with his staff of office. Music played a great part in these festivities which often took place to celebrate the New Year (*Nurūz*) in March. This spring festival was celebrated out of doors then, as it is now, and musicians are shown in miniatures playing the harp (*chang*), lute and *kamāncha* as well as the flute and tambourine, drums and trumpets being more likely to accompany the martial sports such as wrestling, archery and polo.

STORY-TELLING

Gardens and garden pavilions were the venue for story-telling and the recitation of poetry. The Arabian Nights (Thousand and one Nights) is a famous instance of entertainment by the telling of tales and Persian literature has similar works. In Niẓāmī's poem, *Khusraw va Shīrīn*, Shīrīn's maidens tell stories and this is illustrated in a lavish

شده چون لب یار شیرین زبان
همت آب گل چو گل روز در
زکل روی باغ ارغوان بندد
طل مجمول گل برکف دست شاه
دل غنچه چون پسته او بس رنگ
بیا چین علم برگلستان زد
بستاده شمن درجن بسند بنی
چمن پسته و شمن بسند بنی

painting (fig 21) in a manuscript copied and illustrated for Shah Tahmāsp. Under a deep blue night sky full of stars the maidens are clustered near the garden pavilion in which Khusraw and Shīrīn are seated, listening to their tales. The tiled courtyard is lit by candles and the nightwatchman with his lantern lingers listening in the background. In another of Niẓāmī's five poems, the *Haft Paykar* (Seven Portraits) Bahrām Gūr is entertained by the princesses of the seven climes, one for each day of the week. The princesses who were Indian, Moorish, Tartar, Russian, Central Asian, Chinese and Greek each lived in a pavilion of an appropriate colour i.e. black, yellow, green, red, blue, sandalwood and white. All seven pavilions in the *Haft Paykar* are often the subject of miniatures and, less frequently, so are incidents from one or other of the stories.

BATHING

One of these stories concerns a young man who comes home unexpectedly from his travels and finds beautiful maidens bathing in the pool in his garden (fig. 10B). Miniatures of this episode sometimes occur both in Persian and Mughal manuscripts. In some the young man is bashfully watching and in others he is bathing with the girls but in every painting of the subject the artist invariably seizes his opportunity to paint favourite subjects such as lovely women, gardens, water and ornate pavilions.

New Year (*Nurūz*) festivities in Shiraz included bathing in the healing waters in the cisterns below the mausoleum of the Persian poet Saʿdī (d. 1292). Manuscripts of his collected works (*Kulliyāt*) sometimes have a miniature illustrating this scene at the beginning of the manuscript. Shiraz is famous for its poets, gardens, roses and nightingales which are endlessly extolled by one of them, the poet Ḥāfiẓ, and the mausolea of Saʿdī and Ḥāfiẓ are both situated in gardens in Shiraz. Isfahan had extensive gardens too, particularly the Saʿādatābād, a royal garden which used to be at the end of the Chāhār Bāgh. A manuscript (Add. 22789) in the British Library is an illustrated copy of a poem describing the flowers to be found in this garden. Dated 1835 it has thirty paintings of birds, butterflies and, in particular, plants, which include several different roses, Judas-tree blossom, larkspurs, Marvel of Peru (*mirabilis jalapa*), jasmine, amaranthus, irises, tulips and others. *Nurūz* festivities are also illustrated in manuscripts as picnics in the countryside (fig. 11) and one story quite often the subject of miniatures is that of the daughter of the ruler of China being killed by a monster, half-lion, half-ape, whilst picnicking in the country during *Nurūz*.

Turkey, too, delighted in out-door entertainments. The miniatures illustrating these are not in the romantic Persian style but are painted in the more realistic manner of the chronicle illustrators. Most of the festivities described and illustrated are historical and connected with the activities of the Sultan and the palace. Persian artists were taken to Istanbul in the early sixteenth century to teach the palace artists and the style of miniatures dating from this time illustrating poems, stories and epics often reflected those of Persia. Later, however, Turkish artists turned more and more to the illustration of campaigns, palace activities and historical works which required a realistic approach. Festivities were held on special occasions such as the accession of a sultan or circumcision ceremonies or weddings or visits of foreign ambassadors and included fireworks and water displays. Sometimes the trade guilds prepared tableaux and processed before the Sultan with palace officials and naval and military personnel also taking part. In 1582 the Ottoman Sultan, Murad II, held a festival lasting fifty-two days and a manuscript in the Topkapi Saraye Museum Library in Istanbul (the *Sūrnāme*, Book of the Festival) has illustrations of the various guilds not only marching past the Sultan but carrying out their trades as they went. The bakers for instance are shown making bread on a large mobile stove mounted on wheels which is dragged and pushed across the courtyard. Over seven hundred guilds were known to have taken part and must have provided great entertainment to the crowds watching them. There were the executioners with their weapons (in this case not demonstrating their trade), furriers with a cartload of stuffed animals, lion-keepers leading lions on chains, taxidermists carrying huge stuffed birds on poles and bath-house keepers washing people in portable baths, to name a few. Another manuscript in Istanbul also entitled the *Sūrnāme* was produced in the early eighteenth century to celebrate the circumcision of the four sons of Ahmed III (d. 1730) which took place in 1720. These festivities only lasted fifteen days but included a water festival, mock battles, firework displays, dancing, music and acrobatics besides the procession of the guilds. One double-page miniature of the butchers' guild shows the butchers dressed in fur coats, followed by portable butchers' shops and a kebab kitchen on wheels. These *Sūrnāme* manuscripts give a remarkable insight into Turkish recreations as, apart from the procession of the guilds, there are miniatures of dancing, puppets and other amusements as well as games of skill such as archery. Miniatures from these manuscripts are usually on exhibition in the Topkapi Saraye Museum.

Gardens in Turkey were, as in Iran and Mughal India, a great source of pleasure and recreation. Ahmed III's reign was known as the 'Reign of Tulips'. The palace gardens were laid out with tulips, registers were kept of their varieties and many bulbs were imported from Europe. Spring festivals were held in April to celebrate the blossoming of the tulips. It was also during the reign of Ahmed III that the summer houses and gardens of the pashas were built along the shores of the Bosphorus and the Sea of Marmara. The love of flowers is reflected in the designs of tiles and textiles, on carpets and in the cut-out paper pictures of the most intricate nature which are used to ornament Turkish manuscripts.

This subject of pastimes and recreational pursuits must not be concluded without mention of a manuscript called the *Ni'matnāma* or Book of Delicacies which is in the collections of the India Office Library and Records in London. The ruler of Mandu in Western India, Ghiyāth Shāh Khaljī (d. 1500), announced in his accession speech with remarkable candour and good sense that he was going to lay aside the cares of state and give himself up to pleasure. This he proceeded to do by collecting together a bevy of beautiful girls and teaching them the arts of gracious living so that they could entertain him by dancing, singing, recitations, reading aloud, music and cooking his favourite dishes. The manuscript which was written just after Ghiyāth's death in 1500 is in Persian and is a collection of his cookery recipes and prescriptions for medicines, aphrodisiacs, cosmetics and perfume as well as sections on husbandry and hunting. The miniatures reflect the subject-matter and the king is shown, amongst other diversions, teaching girls how to cook various dishes. This and many other manuscripts all down the centuries are proof of the value of miniatures as a record of contemporary life. They also how the diversity of pastimes and recreations in Iran, Turkey and Muslim and Mughal India and the important part they played in the lives of so many people.

This lament by a king bowed down by the cares of state, comes from poem by Nizāmī.

> I should have lived in pleasure, sport and play
> Caressed my soul with music and with wine.

Arberry, A. J. (trans.): *Fifty poems of Hafiz*. Cambridge ,1947

Forster, E. S. (trans.): *The Turkish Letters of Ogier Ghiselin de Busbecq, Imperial Ambassador at Constantinople 1554–1562*. Oxford, 1927

Beveridge, A. S.: *The Babur-nama in English (Memoirs of Babur)*. 2 volumes. London, 1921

Arberry, A. J. (ed.): *The Legacy of Persia*. Oxford, 1953

Lewis, R.: *Everyday Life in Ottoman Turkey*. London, 1971

Wilson, C. E. (trans.): *The Haft Paikar, the life and adventures of Bahram Gur and the seven stories told to him, by Nizami of Ganja*. 2 volumes. London, 1924

Sir John Chardin's Travels in Persia, with an introduction by Sir P. Sykes. London, 1927

Hill, D. R. (trans.): *The Book of Knowledge of Ingenious Mechanical Devices by Ibn al-Razzāz al-Jazarī*. Dordrecht, 1974

Somogyi, S.: *Chess and Backgammon in Ad-Damiri's Hayat al-Hayawan*. Budapest, 1949

Crowe, S. & Haywood, S.: *The Gardens of Mughal India*. London, 1972

Rypka, J.: *History of Iranian Literature*. Dordrecht, 1968

Bell, R. C.: *Board and Table Games from many civilizations*. Oxford, 1960

Warner, A. G. & E. (trans.): *The Shahnama of Firdawsi*. 9 volumes. London, 1905–25

Meredith-Owens, G. M.: *Persian Illustrated Manuscripts*. London, 1973

Meredith-Owens, G. M.: *Turkish Miniatures*. London, 1963

Titley, N. M.: *Miniatures from Persian Manuscripts. A Catalogue and Subject Index of Paintings from Persia, India and Turkey in the British Library and the British Museum*. London, 1977

The last three publications along with wallets of colour transparencies of Persian and Mughal miniatures are available at the Bookshop in the British Museum or from Booksellers.